MW01177965

ONKWEHONWE-NEHA
"Our Ways"

as told by
SKONAGANLEH:RA
(Sylvia Maracle)
Wolf Clan, Mohawk

illustrated by
Carlos Freire

Sister Vision
Black Women and Women of Colour Press

b22794670

Centre

1994 © Copyright Turtle Island Publications
Sylvia Maracle (Skonaganleh:ra)
1994 © Copyright for the Illustrations: Carlos Freire

This book was produced by the collective effort of The Turtle Island Publication Group and
Sister Vision Press

Canadian Cataloguing in Publication Data
Maracle, Sylvia
Onkwehonwe-neha: Mohawk way of life.
ISBN 0-920813-93-3

1. Mohawk Indians – Social life and customs – Juvenile literature.
I. Freire, Carlos, 1943- II.Title. III.Title: Mohawk way of life.
E99.M8M37 1993   j971'.004975   C94-930221-X

Published with the kind assistance of the Canada Council and the Ontario Arts Council

Published by:
Sister Vision Press
P.O. Box 217, Station E
Toronto, Ontario
Canada, M6H 4E2

E
99
M8
M37
1994

ONKWEHONWE-NEHA

"Our Ways"

as told by
SKONAGANLEH:RA
(Sylvia Maracle)
Wolf Clan, Mohawk

illustrated by
Carlos Freire

The Haudenosaunee call themselves *Onkwehonwe* which means "natural human being". According to the beliefs of the Onkwehonwe, any person can become an Onkwehonwe as this word means that we are part of everything and walk in unity and harmony with all that surrounds us.

"Onkwehonwe-neha" means that all life – earth, water, plants, vegetables, trees, animals, rocks, winds, sun, moon, stars, and spirit world are all part of the circle. We are all part of life that the Creator made. It was with great joy and love that the Creator made life. We need only be grateful and thankful for our good life. Everything in life was provided with original instructions – the ways that we would live.

We, as human beings, are the only form of life which has strayed from our original instructions. Our purpose, as the Prophecies revealed, should reflect the relationship we have with the natural and spiritual world. We are each to walk our own path, as the Creator intended.

The relationship that is meant to be maintained between nature and humans is based on mutual respect and harmony. Onkwehonwe-neha refers to the First Peoples' way of life. It includes our languages, ceremonies, education, government and culture. Onkwehonwe-neha could be seen as a basket filled with these things. It was complete. There is no need to go and discover other things because our neha has everything that we need.

The desire of the Onkwehonwe to remain respectful to our instructions was, at one time, part of a wampum belt treaty the Haudenosaunee made with the Dutch who had come to the New World. The *Guswentha*, or the *Two Row Wampum,* set out an agreement which indicated that the Onkwehonwe and the Dutch would travel down a river (life), each group with its own vessel. Each would carry its own laws, language, and ceremonies – their *neha*. This was set out in our treaty – we were not meant to borrow each other's ways or impose our ways on each other.

Yet, in 1867, the Indian Act was passed. The Indian Act took away our neha and replaced it with other ways. The federal government decided that we were to be assimilated and Indian agents were sent to the reserve communities to change our ways to theirs. These Indian agents were white men who had power to make decisions over our lives. For example, when my father was young, he needed the permission of the Indian agent to work outside the community.

The Indian Act made rules to determine who was "Indian" and who was not. In 1951, the Act was changed, yet again, in order to clearly identify just who was an "Indian". The underlying reason for the change was actually to reduce the number of Indian people. The most significant change was to strip Indian status from those women who married non-Indian men. It also took status away from their children. Native women were outraged and fought for the next thirty years to have this racial and sexual discrimination removed from the Indian Act.

In 1946, Ontario revised the Education Act so that all children would attend provincially-recognized schools. The federal government had a long-standing policy of sending Indian children to residential schools administered by religious organizations. Under the new law, it was required that all children, aged six to sixteen, had to attend school. Other provinces followed Ontario's lead which resulted in native children being removed from their communities. The native children went to schools where they learned about *Dick and Jane* and a whole generation grew up looking for *Dick and Jane*. This search further spiralled the children away from our traditions - our neha.

In the 1950's, chiefs in British Columbia organized themselves into a group – this was the beginning of the development of First Nations organizations. There had been organizations prior to this but they were hampered by the Indian Act and its rules about how many Indians could meet in one place "unsupervised", a term indicating that no Indian agents were present.

During the 1960's and 70's, aboriginal people tried to recover our neha. In the 1920's the government, at the urging of the churches, outlawed many traditional ceremonies. In one case, the RCMP raided a longhouse and imprisoned our people which kept them from practising our ways. They were released when the community agreed to elect a band council rather than continue with the traditional council. By the 1960's, some Elders still remembered the old ways but the people generally did not know how to ask the Elders properly for the teachings. Gradually the people recalled what their parents and grandparents had told them about Onkwehonwe-neha.

In 1971, Native Elders collaborated in writing a document called "Indian Control of Indian Education" which laid out what a Native-controlled education system should be. Twenty years later, it has been dusted off and it is still relevant in the debate over education.

So, the 1960's and 70's saw Native people returning to their own ways. The 1970's and 80's brought a consciousness that First Nations had to return to some of the structures that belonged to them. Then came the constitutional process with the First Ministers Conferences on Aboriginal Rights in 1983, 1984 and 1987.

In this process the Canadian government sent a message to the First Nations: they would decide what was in our best interests. The leadership protested this and the result was that First Nations people did become direct participants in the process. There are however, many changes still to be made.

We have moved a long way from our original instructions. To many of our people, our languages, ceremonies and ways are lost. However, not to all. The Creator provided for us a complete way of life. Onkwehonwe-neha is our way. It was the truth thousands of years ago, it is the truth today, and it will be the truth in thousands of years from now. There is a prophecy which foretold of our time of confusion when we would stray from the original instructions. The prophecy also told that we would ultimately have to make a choice about which vessel we will travel in – we continue to be guided by our teachings.

**Other books in this series by the
Turtle Island Publication Group are:**

The Seven Fires: An Ojibway Prophecy
as told by Sally Gaikesheyongai

"Mush Hole": Memories of a Residential School
by Maddie Harper

Other books by First Nations women published by Sister Vision Press

Bird Talk/Bineshiinh Dibaajmowin
by Lenore Keeshig Tobias, illustrated by
Polly Keeshig- Tobais

Beneath the Naked Sun, poetry by Connie Fife

The Invitation, a novel by Cyndy Baskin

*The Colour of Resistance: A Collection of
Contemporary Writing by Aboriginal Women*
anthologised by Connie Fife